One Big Building

A Counting Book About Construction

by **Michael Dahl**

illustrated by **Todd Ouren**

Thanks to our advisers for their expertise, research, and advice:

Stuart Farm, M.A.
Mathematics Lecturer
University of North Dakota
Grand Forks, North Dakota

Susan Kesselring, M.A.
Literacy Educator
Rosemount-Apple Valley-Eagan
(Minnesota) School District

PICTURE WINDOW BOOKS
Minneapolis, Minnesota

The editor would like to thank Donald E. Wolf, P.E.,
for his expert advice in preparing this book.

Managing Editor: Bob Temple
Creative Director: Terri Foley
Editor: Brenda Haugen
Editorial Adviser: Andrea Cascardi
Copy Editor: Sue Gregson
Designer: Nathan Gassman
Page production: Picture Window Books
The illustrations in this book were created digitally.

Picture Window Books
1710 Roe Crest Drive
North Mankato, MN 56003
www.capstonepub.com

Library of Congress Cataloging-in-Publication Data
Dahl, Michael.
One big building : a counting book about construction / written by Michael
Dahl ; illustrated by Todd Ouren.
p. cm. — (Know your numbers)
Summary: A counting book that follows the construction of a building, from
one plan to twelve stories. Readers are invited to find hidden numbers on an
illustrated activity page.
Includes bibliographical references and index.
ISBN-13: 978-1-4048-0580-4 (hardcover)
ISBN-13: 978-1-4048-1120-1 (paperback)
1. Building—Juvenile literature. 2. Counting—Juvenile literature.
[1. Building. 2. Counting. 3. Picture puzzles.] I. Ouren, Todd, ill. II. Title.
TH149 .D34 2004
513.2'11—dc22 [E]   2003020935

Printed in the United States of America in North Mankato, Minnesota.
112016   010148R

ONE big plan for making a big building.

one
1!

Plan   3

TWO shovels dig a giant hole.

two
2

4

THREE dump trucks haul away the dirt.

three
3
...

FOUR pile drivers pound steel into the ground.

6

FIVE concrete mixers rumble and roll.

8

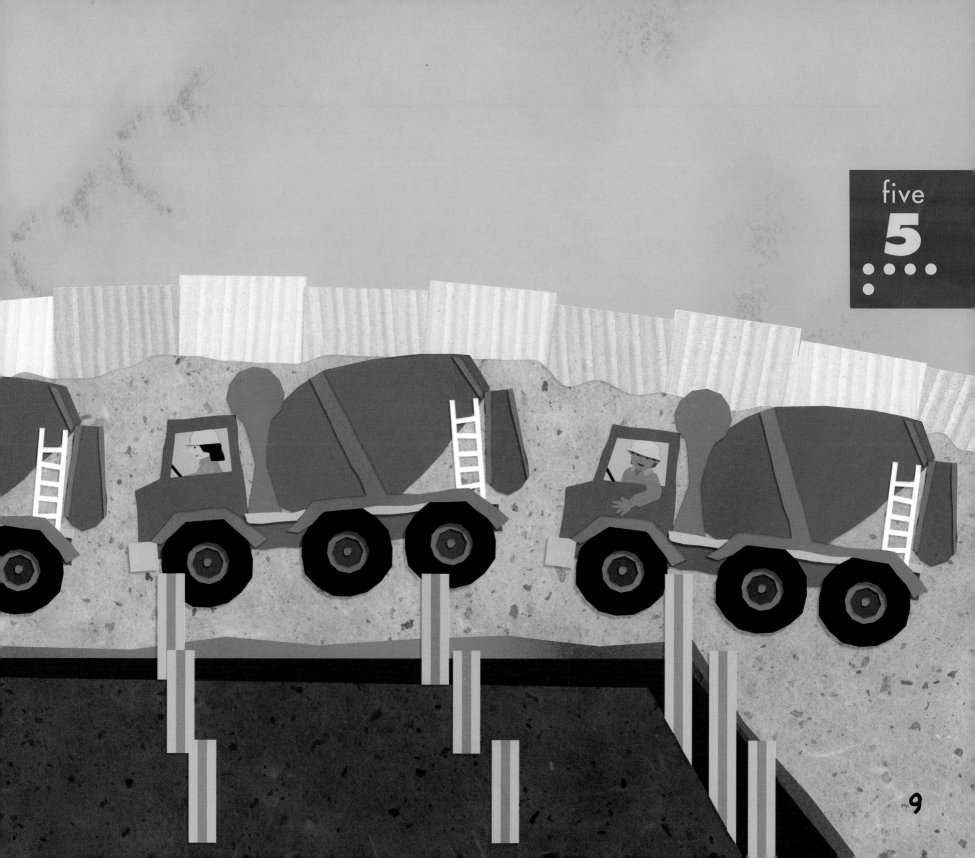

SIX metal beams
are lifted
by a crane.

SEVEN workers sit in the shade and take a break.

EIGHT bosses worry that the weather will turn bad.

NINE wheelbarrows carry supplies.

TEN windows reflect the sky.

ten
10

ELEVEN painters finish the rooms and hallways.

TWELVE stories tall, the new building gleams in the sun.

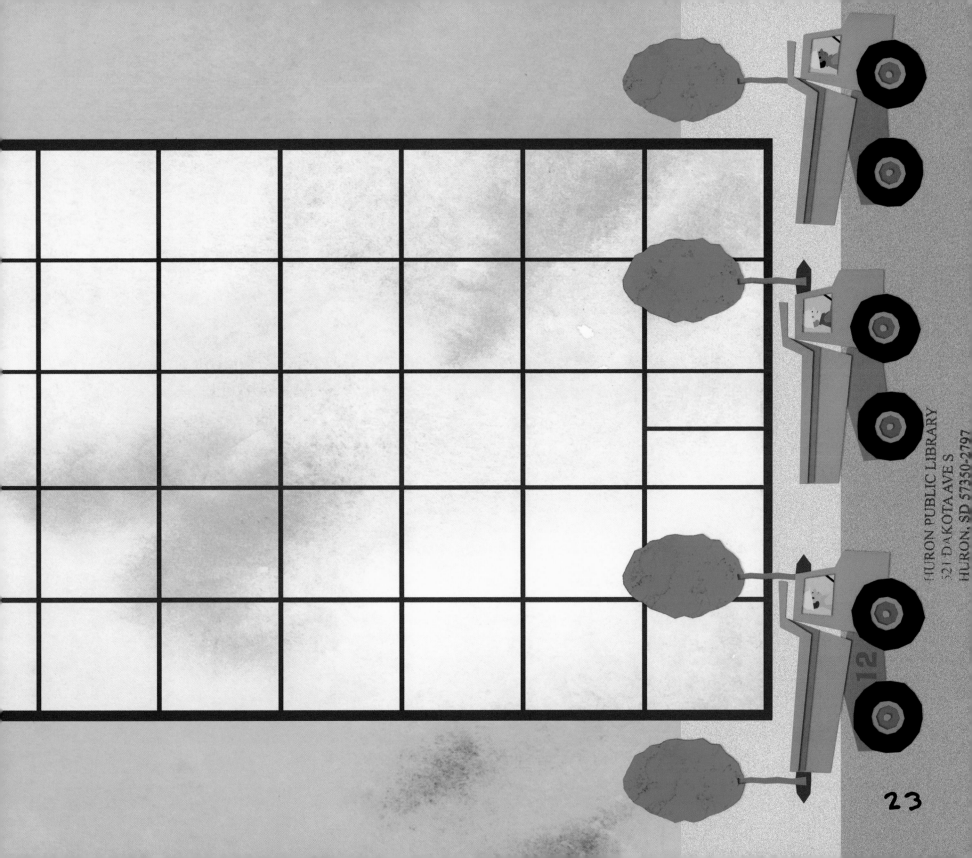

Fun Facts

Before anything can be built, the soil needs to be cleared away for the building's foundation. The foundation supports the whole building!

Almost every building has two main parts. The substructure, or foundation, is the part below the ground. The superstructure is the part above the ground.

The world's tallest free-standing structure is the CN Tower in Toronto, Ontario. This tower is 1,815 feet (533 meters) tall!

The beams of a building are like the bones of your body. Your bones help hold you up. Beams help hold up a building.

Many people are needed to make a building complete. They include carpenters, electricians, plumbers, painters, and many others.

Look for all of the books in the Know Your Numbers series:

Find the Numbers

Now you have finished reading the story, but a surprise still awaits you. Hidden in each picture is one of the numbers from 1 to 12. Can you find them all?

1 —middle window on bottom floor of plan

2 —ready to be scooped up by right shovel

3 —in the front wheel on the farthest right truck

4 —just below the reel for the cable on the pile driver that is farthest left

5 —on the boot of the worker emptying his cement truck

6 —at the top of the crane's cable

7 —the handle of the blue and black drink container

8 —the top of the clipboard the woman is holding on page 1

9 —in the pulley on page 14

10 —on the front of the cart on page 16

11 —on the bottom of the ladder on page 19

12 —between the wheels on the body of the truck that is farthest left

On the Web

FactHound offers a safe, fun way to find Web sites related to this book. All of the sites on FactHound have been researched by our staff.

1. Visit *www.facthound.com*

2. Type in this special code: 140480580X

3. Click on the FETCH IT button.

Your trusty FactHound will fetch the best sites for you!